A
Savannah
Christmas

A Savannah Christmas

KIMBERLY ERGUL & HOLLEY JAAKKOLA

Photography by Richard Leo Johnson

PELICAN PUBLISHING COMPANY
Gretna 2012

Produced by Pinafore Press / Janice Shay
Editing by Sarah Jones
Index by Sara LeVere

Additional photography by:
Christine Hall: pp. 26, 31, 58, 71, 89, 99, 115, 123, 135, 155
Deborah Whitlaw Llewellyn: p. 30
Diane Harvey: pp. 34-37
Wormsloe photos, p. 96-97, courtesy of
Wormsloe State Historic Site

ISBN: 9781455617388
E-book ISBN: 9781455617418

Printed in China

Published by Pelican Publishing Company, Inc.
1000 Burmaster Street, Gretna, Louisiana 70053

To our wonderful husbands,
And precious girls.
—K.E. and H.J.

Contents

A Season by the Sea

Savannah, Georgia and the Low Country set the stage for a perfect Southern holiday season. With very little to no chance of snowflakes falling from the sky, Southerners have their own version of snow, commonly referred to by others as cotton! That "Southern Snow" is used in shop window displays and under Christmas trees for the illusion of a white winter blanket.

December calendars are filled with dates for oyster roasts, holiday parties, and supper with friends. The Southern chapter of hospitality includes presenting neighbors with homemade goodies from the kitchen (packaged appropriately, of course). Casual suppers allow one to finally gain access to friends' family secret holiday recipes, such as Sweet Potato Biscuits and Red Velvet Cake. And, should the weatherman predict temps below 55 degrees, you can bet you'll see several full length mink coats parading around town! Never-the-less, if Mother Nature's temperatures do not call for a roaring fire in the fireplace on Christmas eve, everyone just turns on their air-conditioning to justify those flames.

The city of Savannah has the largest designated Historic District in the United States, but the photographs in this book illustrate much more—they show the wonderful, savory mix of the old and new; all bound together by the rich history. From elegant 150-year-old brownstones, to casual Tybee beach cottages and local shops, this book illustrates the beauty and range of regional holiday decorating, the influence of religious traditions, the grandeur of the coastal landscape and the many different ways Southerners celebrate Christmas.

A Savannah Christmas captures the elegance, traditions, etiquette, and food—as well as, the love and humor—of Savannah and the Low Country. Through photographs of the region, this book allows one to experience a sense of Christmas in this historic Southern city. Savannah and the Low Country are beautiful any time of year, but especially during the season of Christmas.

Happy Holidays, Y'all!

chapter one

The Downtown Historic District

A city founded in 1733, Historic Downtown Savannah is made up of mansions, row houses, brownstones, historic churches, landmarks, parks and squares. Savannah is one of the most beautiful cities in the world, and boasts the largest National Historic Landmark District in the United States. The city's Christmas season is a time of fresh greenery hung on lampposts throughout the squares, shop windows dressed in festive fashion, and special holiday performances. Savannah is a popular travel destination at any time, but it truly "dresses in its finest" at this time of year.

Twenty-Two Squares

Named for U.S. presidents, politicians, heroes, and a religious leader, the downtown Savannah Squares add park-like green spaces to the city's bustling downtown area. The Squares were once destinations for markets and gathering places for the locals.

Residents and business owners who live and work around a square join together to decorate the common space. The early December task has become a social event for everyone involved.

The historic home at right was built in 1844 for silversmith Moses Eastman. It has been used as a residence and a commercial building, and now houses a law firm; however, the tradition of putting a giant Christmas tree on the front porch is lovingly maintained.

Parties are a cherished holiday tradition. Imagine the well-dressed 19th century holiday guests arriving: Men in starched collars and glistening top hats and women in silk and satin gowns as they step down from elegant carriages and sweep happily into the holiday celebrations.

Today, the crystal chandeliers and myriad gas lights remain, as do the sparkling parties, both in homes and on the squares.

Historic Row Houses

Tucked among a row of houses on a brick street is a lovely restored Greek Revival style residence. It was built in 1853, along with five other houses on the same street.

In older American cities, it is customary to decorate with fresh fruit during the holidays. The pineapple is the symbol of hospitality, and is often the centerpiece of a wreath on the front door or in greenery over the top of the door.

Neighbors gather each year to sip cider and sing Christmas carols around the large Christmas tree. Multicolored lights, along with childhood ornaments, glisten like gumdrops.

The homeowners' collection of Christmas carolers is an annual holiday display in the foyer.

White poinsettias and red tapered candles sit upon a hall table made of marble and a concrete balustrade from Egypt.

On the back porch, clementines are piled high on a serving piece.

Citrus is a favorite decorating tool in the South because of its abundance, and it smells incredible. Kumquats and boxwood are tied on one of the decanters in the collection atop an or-nately carved wood and marble chest. White camellia topiaries bring the out-doors in.

The dining table of this house on Jones Street is ready for an elegant can-dlelit dinner and intimate conversation. Silver feathers, white roses, and a sparkly square wreath adorn the man-tel. White roses and lilies are nestled in native grey Spanish moss, which grows in the South's Live Oak trees. Spanish Moss, a plant related to the pineapple family, is often times an accent to Low Country decorations.

These stately townhouses are near Chippewa Square, which was named in 1812 for Canada's Battle of Chippewa. A statue of General James Oglethorpe, the founder of the city of Savannah, is in the center of the square. This square is also known as the setting of the bench scene in the movie *Forrest Gump.* With both history and fame behind the squares, they, too, get dressed up for the holidays.

Wreaths made with fresh fruit are a historically correct decoration for these historic district homes.

Intricate ironwork can be found on many gates and balconies, and in hidden gardens throughout the city. Much of the ironwork is historic, but these gates are by the renowned ironwork artist Ivan Bailey.

The Hamilton Turner House

The Hamilton-Turner house was built for Samuel Pugh Hamilton in 1873. The mid-Victorian mansion was designed by a New York architect. After completion, the impressive residence was known as The Grand Victorian Lady. Currently a bed & breakfast inn, her presence still catches the eye of all who travel around Lafayette Square.

In 1883 electricity was installed in the mansion's salon, and by 1886 the entire house had electric lights. Each evening folks from near and far gathered in Lafayette Square to watch the lights come on at the mansion!

The fireplaces and effacements are of white Italian marble. The coziness of the inn welcomes visitors and displays a festive setting during the holidays.

Savannah is known for her hospitality and wonderful Southern meals. Each morning guests enjoy breakfast, such as Sweet Potato Biscuits with Ham, in this salmon-colored dining room. During the mid-afternoon hours, sweet tea and lemonade are served to the inn's guests, followed by wine and appetizers—before the dinner hour. Prior to bedtime, port wine is available for those staying at the inn.

Sweet Potato Biscuits with Ham

Layer slices of smoked ham onto these flaky biscuits and brush with citrus marmalade while they are still hot. Perfect as a snack for Santa, or for the whole family on Christmas morning!

2 cups self-rising flour
3 tablespoons light brown sugar
¼ cup (1 stick) butter
3 tablespoons shortening
1 cup mashed sweet potatoes
6 tablespoons milk
2 tablespoons butter, melted

Preheat the oven to 400 degrees F. Combine the flour and sugar in a mixing bowl. Using a pastry blender or by hand, cut the butter and shortening into the flour mixture until the mixture is crumbly. Add the sweet potatoes and milk, stirring until all ingredients are thoroughly moistened. Turn the dough out onto a floured surface and roll it out to a 1-inch thickness. Cut the dough with a 2-inch diameter biscuit cutter and place the biscuits onto an ungreased baking sheet. Brush the biscuits with melted butter and bake for 12 minutes.
Yields 15 to 18 biscuits.

Window Shopping

Window shopping is a delightful pastime in downtown Savannah, especially during the holidays. From vintage wares to uptown chic, one can find an array of shops while browsing the historic district.

Shop owners often travel the world to find antiques and one-of-a-kind pieces. Gorgeous monogrammed cocktail napkins, stylish table settings, and the latest runway fashions—downtown Savannah has is all!

This retro Christmas store on Broughton Street was a step into the past for those who were born in the 1950s and 60s—and a treat for anyone who loves pretty things. Many Savannahians count these types of period ornaments as part of their coveted collections.

This lovely old building houses a Christmas store whose windows are decorated year-round for the holidays.

Holiday Inspiration

Located in the center of Richond Hill, Georgia, Ella's is a favorite shop for locals. Named for both the owner's grandmothers, Ella's is a gift boutique as well as a food and flower market. During the month of December the scent of pine adds to the visual array of wrapped gifts, topiaries, and gourmet food from local sources.

The outdoor market offers rows of fresh-cut Christmas trees, holiday flowers, and wreaths in a barn-like setting next door to Ella's gift boutique. The boutique is housed in a 1930s-era cottage.

chapter two

Savannah's Houses of Worship

Savannah is home to a number of historic churches of all denominations. From the distinctive spires of the Cathedral of St. John the Baptist—which represent one of the city's most recognizable features of the city's skyline—to the Wesley Monumental Methodist Church in Calhoun Square, Savannah has long been a welcoming home to congregations and followers of all faiths. This is even more apparent during the holiday season. Heavenly music floats out of houses of worship, such as this philharmonic Christmas concert at the cathedral, where the song and music in the spirit of the season is a meaningful and unforgettable experience.

Cathedral of St. John the Baptist

One of the most beautiful historic sites in Savannah, the Cathedral of St. John the Baptist, overlooks Lafayette Square. The Parish of St. John the Baptist dates from 1799, and its structure is 15,856 square feet with the capacity to seat 1,000 people. The gorgeous windows came from Innsbruck, Austria.

During the Christmas season, the sanctuary is adorned with a giant poinsettia Christmas tree and a treasured nativity scene complete with lights, waterfalls, and flying angels. One of the church's seasonal highlights is the Christmas Eve midnight mass.

Wesley Monumental United Methodist

Standing tall on the west side of Calhoun Square is Wesley Monumental United Methodist Church.

The structure is a monument to John and Charles Wesley, founder of the Methodist movement. The first phase of the church building was completed on May 12, 1878. It is in the Gothic architectural style with spires, or steeples, measuring 136 and 196 feet in height.

The sanctuary features a magnificent Noack organ and has a soaring ceiling 43 feet tall. Each December, the Altar Guild participates in the "hanging of the greens." Fresh balsam garland, vibrant red poinsettias, and Christmas trees adorn the sanctuary in celebration of the Advent and Christmas season.

First Unitarian Universalist: The Jingle Bells Church—

The popular yuletide song "Jingle Bells" was composed by James Lord Pierpont sometime in the 1850s for the church choir at this Unitarian Church. The tune was written for the Thanksgiving season; and was so popular it was performed again at the Christmas services, and many times since by people all over the world.

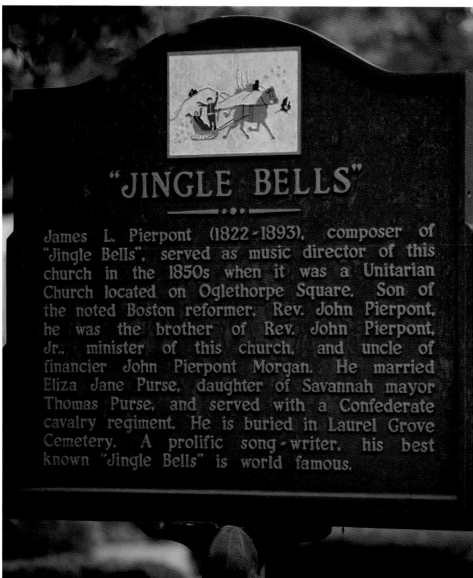

"JINGLE BELLS"

James L. Pierpont (1822-1893), composer of "Jingle Bells", served as music director of this church in the 1850s when it was a Unitarian Church located on Oglethorpe Square. Son of the noted Boston reformer, Rev. John Pierpont, he was the brother of Rev. John Pierpont, Jr., minister of this church, and uncle of financier John Pierpont Morgan. He married Eliza Jane Purse, daughter of Savannah mayor Thomas Purse, and served with a Confederate cavalry regiment. He is buried in Laurel Grove Cemetery. A prolific song-writer, his best known "Jingle Bells" is world famous.

St. John's Episcopal Church

St. John's Episcopal Church was consecrated on May 7, 1853. The Gothic Revival architecture was designed by Calvin Otis. The Green-Meldrim 1850s mansion and garden is located next to the church. It was purchased in 1943 for use as the Parrish House and Rectory.

One of the holiday highlights for this congregation and other Savannahians is the annual Holly Days Bazaar. The bazaar offers handmade crafts, ornaments, unique one-of-a-kind objects, and canned jellies and jams. In addition, a delicious lunch is served consisting of a menu of soups, pimento cheese, shrimp salad sandwiches, and yummy desserts.

Bethesda Chapel

Upon their arrival to Georgia in 1738, George Whitefield and James Habersham recognized the need for a place to nurture and teach poor children. Bethesda was established as an orphanage in 1740. It remains in operation today as a school for boys, renamed Bethesda Academy. The school is situated on a large amount of acreage beside the Moon River.

In 1916, the chapel's cornerstone was laid by the National Society of Colonial Dames of America in Georgia. The building was completed in 1925, and was officially presented to Bethesda in 1930. In memory of George Whitefield, the chapel is a reproduction of his church in England.

chapter three

The Ardsley Park Neighborhood

Developed in 1910, Ardsley Park was Savannah's first automobile suburb. The neighborhood streets are lined with live oaks, crape myrtles, magnolia trees, and palms. During Christmas, the homes (ranging from Greek Revival mansions to simple Craftsman bungalows) gleam with their own personality of decorating. The neighborhood's Christmas tree is front and center in Kavanaugh park, facing Savannah's main thoroughfare. Neighbors gather the first Sunday of December to watch the tree light up, enjoy a trolley ride while singing Christmas carols, and of course, have a chat with the man in red.

Entertaining, Tudor-style

From sunrise to sunset to moonlight, a porch is an extension of a Low Country home. This outdoor space has a merry holiday ambiance. White poinsettias, a moss-wrapped gift, and white twinkle lights make for a perfect setting to entertain guests. The homeowners have hung square shaped wreaths, rather than traditional round ones, on each of the porch posts.

Breakfast in the garden can be enjoyed year-round in the Low Country. Clusters of beautiful burgundy amaryllis stand at attention in the background.

The interior of this Ardsley Park home is Neoclassical and Old World style. The iron gates, leading into the living room from the foyer, were created by a local ironsmith. The hue of the holiday decoration creates a serene atmosphere.

Savannahians consider their pets full-fledged family members. The family beagle, Juniper (above), has her very own Christmas tree with edible doggie treat ornaments.

Ardsley's First Home

Ardsley Park was developed around 1910. Located only a few short miles from the downtown district, the invention of the automobile allowed local residents to move to this first suburban community.

This Washington Avenue home was the first in Ardsley Park, and it remains one of the grandest in Savannah. The 1920 mansion proudly sits among moss-draped oaks at the corner of two main streets. With Edwardian architecture and massive columns, the residence was built for Henry Hays Lattimore, one of the developers of the Ardsley Park neighborhood.

The mantel (far right) is adorned with birds and Christmas trees constructed of peacock feathers. The self-supporting, curved staircase (right) is an engineering accomplishment created entirely of wood.

Going Green

Built in 1913, this Ardsley Park Craftsman style residence is simply decorated to reflect its clean architecture lines.

A wooden basket holds an indoor garden of white amaryllis, paper whites, maidenhair fern, English ivy, and rex begonia. On the mantle are paper whites planted in oriental vases.

The ball of mistletoe (right) not only calls for a kiss from those passing underneath, but—according to the Norse legend—brings good luck and fertility

Lancaster Tree Farm

A family holiday tradition is traveling to the Lancaster Christmas tree farm and chopping down their own Christmas tree. One December, a local family's minister even came over to their home and blessed the tree! Leland Cypress, Eastern Red Cedar, and Virginia Pine are grown as Christmas trees in Georgia and South Carolina.

Holiday Dinner with Friends

This sunroom is the perfect setting for a casual holiday dinner with friends. Taking a break from dressy parties and soirees, friends feel relaxed in this simple, but elegant, space.

Guests are allowed to help themselves to local steamed stone crab claws, lump blue crab, shrimp and oysters on the sideboard. A mignonette, cocktail sauce, and creamy mustard sauce are traditionally served with seafood in the Low Country style.

Two farm tables nestle together, set with antique China, linen, napkins, and tiny glass vases filled with Star-of-Bethlehem blossoms.

Sea whips (left) , gathered from Little Tybee Island, are mounted and displayed on the wall in shadow boxes. Coral, clusters of oyster shells, and local artwork makes a lovely sideboard tableau.

Pickled Shrimp

Susan Mason created this recipe. It has become a holiday favorite for the luxurious parties she caters during the holidays and on special occasions year-round.

2 ½ pounds (21 to 26) large shrimp,
peeled, deveined, tails removed
2 stalks celery, chopped
½ cup sliced onions
1 ½ cups chopped green bell pepper
1 ¼ cups vegetable oil
¾ cup apple cider vinegar
1 ½ teaspoons salt
7 to 8 bay leaves
2 ½ tablespoons capers, with juice
6 to 7 drops Tabasco sauce

Bring a large pot of salted water to a boil, drop the shrimp in, and reduce to a simmer. Cook the shrimp in simmering water for 3 to 5 minutes, or until pink. Drain well. In a 2-quart glass container, combine the shrimp, celery, onion, bell peppers, oil, vinegar, salt, bay leaves, capers and juice, and Tabasco. Cover and chill for 24 hours, stirring occasionally.

Drain the liquid just before serving and remove the bay leaves. Serve with party picks or as a buffet dish. Serves 8 to 10.

The Santa Trolley

At an annual gathering in Ardsley Park, Santa arrrives by trolley to celebrate the start of the holiday season. Carolers—both adults and children—ride the trolley around Ardsley Park singing their favorite carols—a beloved neighborhood event that everyone enjoys.

Natural Beauty

Decorating in this semi-tropical climate allows Savannahians to use an abundance of greenery, fruits, and flowers that are available locally. Wreaths of magnolia leaves hang above mantels and wrap stair rails, blooming plants and forced bulbs are readied for the season, and the sparkle of lights is often replaced with the colors of nature.

This topiary decorated with confederate Jasmine and green Granny Smith apples. It serves as a beautiful—and edible—centerpiece.

An inviting porch and window boxes with displays of holly and berries make this Federal-style home in Ardsley Park a treat for holiday guests. Festive pots of poinsettias and fresh greenery give guests a taste of the festive atmosphere inside.

The mantle (below) is dressed with viburnum branches, pomegranates, key limes, and fragrant white lilies.

The potting shed is a place to relax and create. Palm fronds, camellias, Phalaenopsis orchids, and amaryllis are the supplies for all sorts of beautiful creations.

This industrious gardener thinks ahead so that all her flowering bulbs are ready for the season. The potting shed serves as a nursery as well as a greenhouse, and the space is a lovely preview of her holiday flowers.

This little Rudolph stands sentry at the window, with tiny candles lighting the way for Santa's sleigh to find him by Christmas eve, no doubt.

This large live tree in Kavanaugh Park is decorated annually by the Ardsley Park Neighborhood Association with help from the children.

Back in the Day Bakery

Close to Ardsley, in a small neighborhood known as Starland, is a well-known and much loved bakery specializing in all things handmade and delicious. (Think butter cream icing, heavenly cupcakes, and the feeling that you've just stepped back into your childhood.) The eclectic owners are frequent guests on the Food Network, and Paula Deen is one of their best clients, proving the adage "everything old is new again." The aroma of fresh baked breads, homemade brownies, and beautifully iced cakes greets you at the door.

Chocolate-Covered Cherry Cookies

1 ½ cups all-purpose flour
½ cup unsweetened cocoa powder
1 cup sugar
¼ teaspoon salt
¼ teaspoon baking powder
¼ baking soda
½ cup butter (room temperature)
1 egg
1 ½ teaspoon vanilla
24 maraschino cherries, drained, and juice saved
1 (6 ounce) package semi-sweet chocolate chips
½ cup sweetened condensed milk

Combine the flour and cocoa in a small bowl and set aside. In a separate large mixing bowl, beat the butter with an electric mixer on medium speed until softened. Add the sugar, salt, baking powder, and baking soda and beat until well mixed. Add the egg and vanilla. Gradually beat in the flour mixture. Shape the dough into 1-inch balls and place on an ungreased baking sheet. Press down the center of each ball with your thumb. Place a cherry in the center of each cookie.

To make the frosting, in a small saucepan combine the chocolate chips and sweetened condensed milk. Stir the chocolate over low heat until it has melted. Gradually stir in 4 teaspoons of the reserved cherry juice. Spoon about 1 teaspoon of the frosting over half of each cherry (it makes a prettier cookie to see half of the cherry). Bake at 350 degrees F for 10 minutes. Cool cookies on a wire rack. Yields 2 dozen.

Ladyfingers

1 cup plus 2 tablespoons all-purpose flour
½ cup butter, softened
½ cup chopped pecans
¼ cup sifted powder sugar
1/2 teaspoon vanilla

Powdered sugar, for rolling

Cream the butter with an electric mixer. Add ¼ cup sifted powdered sugar. Add in flour, pecans, and vanilla and stir to combine. Form into a small log and bake at 400 degrees F for 10 to 12 minutes. Roll the cookies in powdered sugar and cool completely on wire racks. Yields 2 dozen.

Cheese Straws

2 cups (8 ounces) shredded cheese
½ cup butter, softened
1 ½ cups all-purpose flour
1 teaspoon paprika
½ teaspoon salt
½ teaspoon red pepper

Combine the cheese and butter; beat well at medium speed with an electric mixer. Combine the remaining ingredients and add slowly to cheese mixture.

Using a cookie gun, form the cheese straws according to manufacturer's instructions, or roll the dough out 1/3-inch thickness and cut into 2 x ½-inch strips using a sharp knife or a pastry wheel. Preheat the oven to 375 degrees F and bake for 10 to 12 minutes. Yields 8 dozen.

Variation: ## Pinwheels with Mayhaw Jelly

Roll the dough to 1/3-inch thickness in the shape of a rectangle. Spread a thin layer of strawberry fig preserves or mayhaw jam or jelly on top of the dough. Sprinkle with ½ cup finely chopped pecans. Roll the dough up like a jelly roll, wrap with plastic wrap, and refrigerate for one hour. Slice and bake at 375 degrees F for 10 to 12 minutes. (See photo, bottom right.)

Gingerbread with Meyer Lemon Glaze

1 cup flour
½ cup millet flour

1 teaspoon baking soda
½ teaspoon cinnamon
½ teaspoon ground ginger
¼ teaspoon nutmeg
¼ teaspoon ground cloves
1 stick butter
¼ cup milk
½ cup molasses
3 eggs
1 teaspoon vanilla
1 (2-inch) piece of ginger, grated and peeled
1/3 cup powdered sugar, optional
¼ cup Meyer lemon juice

Preheat the oven to 350 degrees F. Lightly grease a loaf pan. In a medium bowl, sift together the flour, baking soda, spices and salt. Set aside. In a microwavable bowl, melt the butter and milk together in the microwave. Set aside. In a mixer, combine the molasses, eggs, and vanilla. Beat slowly until combined. Add dry ingredients and then pour in the melted butter. Mix together, then add fresh grated ginger. Pour the batter into a pan and bake 40 minutes. Allow to cool before you glaze.

In a small bowl, combine the powdered sugar and Meyer lemon juice. Allow the mixture to thicken slightly in the bowl, then pour over the top of the gingerbread.

Lace Cookies

1 ¼ sticks unsalted butter
1 cup dark brown sugar
¼ cup light corn syrup
1 tablespoon heavy cream
1 teaspoon vanilla
¼ teaspoon salt
¼ cup all-purpose flour
1 ¼ cups old-fashioned rolled oats

Preheat the oven to 350 degrees F. Line a cookie sheet with parchment paper. Melt the butter over low heat. Remove from the heat and stir in the brown sugar, stirring until it is dissolved. Add the corn syrup, cream, vanilla, and salt. Stir in the flour and oats. Drop the dough onto a cookie sheet by rounded teaspoonfuls, 3 inches apart. Bake for 6 to 7 minutes, or until the edges are slightly dark. Allow the cookies to cool in the pan. Store in airtight container.

Glittering Gumdrops

Baking and decorating sugar cookies is a favorite family tradition for the two young daughters in this family. A Noah's Ark theme is created with animals of every shape and size. The creatures are hung on the dining room Christmas tree, a centerpiece terrarium houses several of the animals, and a single animal cookie is placed on each plate around the table. Penguins, giraffes, and other animal-shaped cookies fill the terrarium. The children enjoy creating non-traditional colored animals during the holidays. The cookies are able to stand up-right by filling the bottom of the terrarium with mounds of sugar or rock salt.

To honor her grandmother's gumdrop tree tradition in her own home, the homeowner cuts oak tree branches and tops the tips with colorful candy gumdrops. The tree limbs are then tucked into the branches of the Christmas tree and woven throughout the chandelier.

Sugar Cookies

1 cup butter, softened
1½ cups 4X powdered sugar, sifted
1 egg
1 teaspoon vanilla
2½ cups all-purpose flour
1 teaspoon baking soda
1 teaspoon cream of tartar
Sugar crystals, optional

Royal Icing
3 tablespoons Meringue Powder
4 cups (1 pound) confectioners' sugar
6 tablespoons warm water

In a mixing bowl, cream the butter and gradually add the powdered sugar, blending until the mixture is light and fluffy. Add the eggs and vanilla and beat well. In a separate bowl, combine the flour, baking soda, and cream of tartar. Add this to the mixture, beating well. The dough should be soft. Cover and chill at least 3 hours.

Work with half the dough at a time, keeping the remaining dough chilled. Roll the dough to a ¼-inch thickness and cut with cookie cutters. Place the cookies on a lightly greased baking sheet and bake at 375 degrees F for 10 minutes, or until they are a light golden-brown color.

To make the royal icing, beat all the ingredients in an electric mixer on high speed for 10 to 12 minutes, or until peaks form. If you want to color your icing, add a few drops of food coloring to the bowl and mix until the color is consistent. If you want to make several colors, divide the icing into seaparte bowls, add a different color to each bowl, and mix well.

chapter four

Hanukkah in Habersham Woods

Nestled between Savannah's mid-town and the Southside area of the city is the Habersham Woods neighborhood. It features 1960s and 1970s homes of both traditional Savannah grey brick and modern architecture. A large Jewish population resides in the area due to the close proximity of the local synagogues. The community embraces the season of Hanukkah with great pride in their heritage, reflected here in their beautiful tables.

A silver Menorah (left) secures the napkin on a gold-rimmed china plate with charger. The table is layered with green fatsia leaves, orange clementines, and scattered with dreidels and gold coins.

Menorahs, collected over many years, create a warm glow and special memories for this family. The dining room features a beautiful silver tea service on the buffet, a Southern signature.

[chapter five]

The Isle of Hope

Isle of Hope is just one narrow river bridge away from Savannah's other communities. As one resident once said, "But it is a quarter mile and a world away from the continental United States." A paved road languidly follows the gentle curves of the Skidaway River. Wide front porches are draped with garland. Gas lanterns secured with large bows burn bright. Carolers travel in groups from house to house singing Christmas favorites. Across the river, you can see islands dotted with marsh and palm trees. During high tide, deer swim through the cold tidal creeks back to the main island. Walking down Bluff Drive, one of the most picturesque streets in America, you know you are somewhere special. Three hundred year live oaks line the drive as residents catch Atlantic blue crab on their docks and enjoy the river and the breezes it blows across the island. Tiny Christmas lights wrap the warm weather docks to remind everyone it is December! Children love to ride bikes to the marina to buy ice cream and explore the island. When it is time to come home, parents ring a large bell on their back porch.

Established in 1736, the name 'Isle of Hope' came from the colonists' hope for prosperity in the new land. Overlooking the Skidaway River, this neighborhood island is known for wonderful community spirit and charm.

In the early 20th century, the island the year-round home of many, and the terrapin farm at Barbee's Pavillion became world famous for the export of terrapins for stew, including to the major restaurants of New York City and to the Czar of Russia. This delicacy was on the Christmas menu at many Isle of Hope homes on Christmas Eve. It was also the destination of dashing race car drivers from around the world for the International Grand Prix races.

Palm Fronds and Starfish

What was once a marine supply house is now a beautiful residence on the Isle of Hope. The 1904 structure has an oil stain on the wood floor that reflects its history.

The front door opens to reveal urns filled with long leaf pines, native palm fronds and citrus. A single starfish is placed within the garland above the door. Soft light glows from the iron lanterns.

Decorated for the holidays, this handsome home portrays elegance and simplicity. The pecky cypress mantel (above) is arranged with cedar, pine, palms and saw grass clipped from around the island. Filled with red and silver ornaments, starfish, and burgundy kangaroo paw branches, the floral compositions reflect the island's indigenous growth.

On the stair rail is a large palm frond, cut from the garden and anchored by gold ribbon, ornaments, Frasier fir and cedar garland. A chest in the background is covered with seashells from all over the world and draped with long leaf pine.

Original art by local artists, oyster shell-framed mirrors, and silver bowls punctuate the serenity of this Isle of Hope home at the holidays.

Five Generations and Growing

Savannah's poinsettias are almost all grown at one locale, Oelschig Nursery. It is a family business run by the fifth generation of Oelschig's and they take great pride in their calling. They start growing in July to have the 40,000-plus plants ready for the holidays, all of them nurtured in a 120,000 square foot greenhouse.

The Oelschig family grows around 15 types of poinsettias that are fit for this climate and cover the color spectrum of hybrids.

Grandfather George savors a moment with his grandson Christian. With so many generations of Oelschigs working in the business, it's a certainty that the green thumb is passed on from generation to generation!

Serenity on the River

One of the first homes on the island, this Isle of Hope home was originally constructed in 1720 to house the gatekeepers for Noble Jones' estate, the nearby Wormsloe Plantation. The home has been enjoyed by families for generations.

The front porch is original to the house, as are the windows in the dining room. The kitchen cabinets are made from the original pine flooring. The circa 1720-era home's interior is

now classic contemporary. Holiday decorations complement the elegant surroundings—they are simple, yet worldly. Celebrating Hanukkah, this family keeps the light shining. With lit snowflakes swaying in the humid breeze, the home is just steps away from the Intracoastal Waterway.

Crab Stew

This is a recipe by Martha Nesbit, one of Savannah's star chefs and cookbook authors.

6 tablespoons (¾ stick) butter
1 cup green onions roughly cut
½ cup celery, roughly chopped
1 (2-inch) piece of carrot
6 tablespoons flour
2 ½ cups milk
2 ½ cups chicken broth,
preferably homemade
¼ teaspoon nutmeg
¼ teaspoon white pepper
⅛ teaspoon cayenne pepper
1 cup cream
¼ cup sherry
1 pound claw crab meat,
picked through for shells

Melt the butter over low heat in a saucepan. Mince the green onions, celery, and carrot in a food processor, or by hand. Add the vegetables to the butter, cover the saucepan, and sauté over low heat for 5 minutes. Whisk in the flour and cook for 2 minutes more to remove the starchy taste. Whisk in the milk and broth. Bring to a boil, whisking occasionally. Add seasonings, cream, sherry, and crab and mix.

If you're not serving immediately, refrigerate in an airtight container. Reheat over very low heat until very hot. Serves 12.

On the Dock

Bluff Drive on Isle of Hope is considered one of Savannah's most beautiful streets. Walking down the 'Bluff' in December, you'll enjoy the white picket fences draped with garland, and beautiful front porches and wooden docks strung with twinkle lights.

Residents enjoy fishing and crabbing from their docks year round. Families gather on lush, green lawns to have crab boils and oyster roasts. Neighbors know how to celebrate holidays the Low Country way.

Wormsloe Plantation

The entrance to Wormsloe Plantation is an iconic image for Savannah locals and visitors, used in numerous movies and on book covers. The 1½- mile-long oak alley of this historic site leads to the old plantation house museum. A nature trail leads walkers past the tabby ruins of a home that dates back to the 1700s.

While the Wormsloe mansion (below) is quite grand, it is also welcoming. The current full-time residents—family descendants—celebrate holidays and special occasions at the residence. Holiday decorations are mostly flowers, ribbons, and greenery, to match the 18th-century traditions of this beautiful historic home.

The portrait over the mantel (opposite page) is of Lieutenant Colonel Lewis Stevenson Craig, the homeowner's great-great-grandfather who was killed in 1852 by deserters of the United States militia. His wife was the daughter of Alonzo Church of Athens, Georgia, who was an early leader of the University of Georgia.

A kumquat-studded boxwood topiary on the mantel is an example of how Southerners love to decorate with the bountiful citrus available during the holidays. Large candy cane camellias, pine needles, magnolia branches, and holly fern from the garden also drape the mantel.

The old garden at Wormsloe displays mature creeping fig vines that have covered the brick walls.

A stone bunny stands watch over the winter garden.

A Colonial Christmas

It was 1733 when General James Edward Oglethorpe founded the Georgia colony, and a surveyor named Noble Jones was granted some land on the island that was named Wormsloe.

Now the residents of this special island community and the surrounding areas help the season's magic come alive at the annual Colonial Christmas celebration. Every year at the Wormsloe Historic Site, families and friends gather together to commemorate the season in Colonial fashion—literally. Traditions from the time of the colony's founding are kept alive through this spirited custom, complete with caroling, period costumes, dancing to live music, games, and food that reflect the lifestyles of those who lived in the area during the 18th century.

Living history demonstrations and the lighting of the Yule log gives participants a taste of what life would have been like when General James Edward Oglethorpe first arrived on the shores of Georgia's coast.

Mile High Red Velvet Cake

2½ cups cake flour, sifted
1 teaspoon baking powder
1 teaspoon salt
2 tablespoons cocoa powder
2 ounces red food coloring
½ cup (2 sticks) butter, softened
1½ cups sugar
2 eggs
1 teaspoon vanilla
1 cup buttermilk
1 teaspoon white vinegar
1 teaspoon baking soda

Cream Cheese Frosting
2 (8-ounce) packages cream cheese
¼ cup (1 stick) butter, room temperature
1 pound powdered sugar, sifted
1 pound finely chopped pecans, optional

Preheat the oven to 350 degrees F. Spray and line 2 (8-inch) backing pans. Sift together the flour, baking powder, and salt; set aside. In a small bowl, mix the food coloring and cocoa to form a thin paste without lumps and set aside. In the bowl of a mixer, cream the butter and sugar together for three minutes. Beat in the eggs one at a time. Add the vanilla and red cocoa paste, scraping down with a spatula as you go. Add the flour mixture alternatively with the buttermilk to the butter mixture. Beat until combined. In a small bowl, mix the vinegar and baking soda together. Be careful—this mixture will fizz. Add this to the cake mixture and mix to combine. Divide evenly between cake pans and bake at 350 degrees F until a cake tester or a toothpick inserted in the center comes out clean. Turn the cakes out of the pans onto cooling racks and cool completely. When cool, cut each layer in half to make 4 layers, or cut into thirds to make 6 layers. Frost the cake generously between layers and on all sides with cream cheese frosting.

To make the frosting, cream together the butter and cream cheese until smooth. Add the vanilla. Slowly add the sifted sugar to the creamed mixture. (For a stiffer and sweeter frosting, an additional pound of powdered sugar can be added to the frosting mixture.)

chapter six

Tybee Island

Eighteen miles east of Savannah, Tybee Island is a small barrier island that hosts a three-mile long beach with a backdrop of sea-oat covered sand dunes. Native Americans who originally lived on this barrier island named it Tybrisa, which means salt. The short version, Tybee Island, has stuck, but many older residents still refer to it as Tybrisa.

Screen doors slamming, hammocks in motion, and children enjoying the outdoors means it is Christmas break on the island. December at the beach translates into antique silver tinsel Christmas trees with a starfish gracing the top. An oyster pit lined with shells from past roasts paves the way for families and neighbors to gather in the backyard. Warmer temperatures and sandy beaches offer a refuge from the city during the winter months. While many Tybee residents enjoy their Christmas decorations year round, December is truly a time for celebration.

Driving over the Lazaretto Creek bridge, visitors and residents are greeted by a favorite smalltown tradition: lit snowflakes and anchors glowing from the street lamps. Tybee's main street, Butler Avenue, offers a glimpse of Santa in a swimsuit enjoying an icy cocktail.

Over a cup of hot crab stew at a dockside restaurant overlooking the back river, locals gather to have dinner and watch the dolphins as the sun sets.

The island's south end pier and pavilion is great for people watching, strolling and fishing. Tybee hosts the Polar Bear Plunge on January 1st, with locals jumping into the chilly water to celebrate the first day of the New Year. This island is home to colorful characters, wooden beach cottages, island traditions, and beautiful beaches.

Amazing Grace Cottage

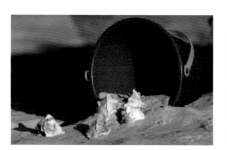

Situated on an acre of land overlooking the back river of Tybee Island, this lush landscape is filled with fragrant ginger, Raphael Blue hydrangeas, citrus and banana trees. An expansive porch, filled with hanging beds, hammocks and comfortable antique wicker sofas and chairs, offers views of sloping sand dunes, the ocean, and Little Tybee Island.

A chartreuse, white, and butter yellow lady slipper orchid (opposite page)

A collection of mercury glass shimmers on the table. Breakfast muffins are served along with traditional gingerbread cookies. An oyster shell chandelier, constructed by a Tybee artist, adds rustic glamour to this table. A dazzling silver tree (opposite page), handmade treasures, and a whimsical painting give this room a feeling of holiday fun.

is planted in a vintage polka-dot tin. A homemade dark fruitcake studded with fruits and nuts is baked in late October, wrapped in cheesecloth, and drizzled with peach brandy once a week until it is ready to serve in December.

Ticket Booth Cottage

The Ticket Booth cottage, a one-room guesthouse located behind the main cottage—named Lucious Little cottage—is a perfect place for children to spend the night during the holidays.

The Ticket Booth was once part of the railway system that brought visitors from the mainland. It is screened on all sides, which lets in the breezes on hot summer days.

It also now serves as a wonderful sleeping porch, a tradition in the South that dates back to the time before air conditioning.

Little Palm Cottage

Little Palm cottage was built in the early 1930's to house road workers. After decades of disrepair, it was slated to be razed. In 1998, a visionary purchased the house for one dollar, relocated the cottage to its current site on Tybee, and refurbished it.

The bright, citrus-colored green doors, turquoise shutters and morning-glory-blue wooden steps leading to the front door made this one of the first cottages painted in the now iconic pastel "Tybee style."

The simple magnolia swag on the front door is tied with a matching citron ribbon to welcome visitors. The table (below) is ready for a children's holiday party.

Little Palm Cottage is cozy and charming. A built-in banquette allows for more seating when neighboring children drop by for a delicious surprise. With the table set in muted blue polka-dotted plates and deliciously pretty holiday cookies, the atmosphere is magical!

Tybee's cottages are dedicated to casual comfort, which means you won't find one without a hammock. And it's unusual to find an empty hammock like this one—there's always someone ready to relax after a long day of Christmas shopping, then checking out the light displays on the island!

A Southern Point of View

An east coast family calls this incredible cottage home. With sweeping views of the Atlantic Ocean, it is the ideal place to reconnect with family and friends. From this porch on the southern tip of the island, they can see people shelling, flying kites, windsurfing and kayaking.

With a small Christmas tree dressed up with shiny beads and citron yellow ilex branches, this spectacular porch is ready for Christmas.

The centerpiece (opposite page, left) for this holiday table is a wreath made of pine, fir, and wispy sea grasses. To add a coastal reference, the wreath is anchored with an oyster shell base.

A color palette of tropical orange and ocean blue throughout the house creates a sense of place and introduces a few unexpected colors in the holiday decor.

The topiary angel resting on an old garden bench was created by using fresh moss over an angel form, and then planted with English ivy. Her wings and halo are made of 10 gauge wire.

A boxwood wreath strung with key limes hangs on the icebox of this vintage turquoise kitchen.

Coffee Punch

4 cups brewed coffee
12 ounces evaporated milk
¼ cup sugar
½ gallon vanilla ice cream, softened
Marshmallows
Peppermints

In a large bowl, combine the coffee, milk, sugar, and ice cream and stir until the sugar is dissolved. Pour into coffee cups. Sprinkle with marshmallows and peppermints.

Chatham Artillery Punch

Savannah's most famous drink, this original concoction was created over 200 years ago as the house punch of the Chatham County Artillery of Savannah, formed May 1, 1786. It was originally brewed in ice-filled horse buckets. Stir 1 pound of green tea into 2 gallons of water. Soak overnight in a tin bucket and strain. To the green tea, add the juice of 3 dozen lemons, preferably using a cedar tub. Then add five pounds of brown sugar, 2 gallons of Catawba wine, 2 gallons of rum, 1 gallon of brandy, 1 gallon of dry gin, and 1 gallon of whiskey. Allow the mixture to sit for 1 or 2 weeks in a covered container. When ready to serve, pour the liquid over ice cubes or a cake of ice. (Never chill in the refrigerator or use crushed ice.) Add 2 quarts cherries, 2 quarts pineapple cubes and 10 quarts champagne, pouring each ingredient in slowly and stirring with a circular motion. The punch, which serves 200, is ready to do its damage.

A Mermaid Cottage ⁓

This authentic retro kitchen is the place to find fresh baked cookies and treats during the holidays. A treasured Santa chef figurine is displayed each year.

The white, ethereal stairwell (far right), illuminated with candles, is punctured by the soothing colors of a blue crab painting by a local artist, and jewel-like drops hang

down from a vintage chandelier—purchased at a favorite shop—gleam both day and night.

A footed bathtub (below) offers a relaxing soak and respite from the busy holiday season. Renovated in 1990, this house shows off vintage kitchen and bathrooms updated with modern conveniences.

chapter seven

Other Islands & Hammocks

Luxurious homes, golf courses, bike trials, wild creatures, and thousands of palms can be found on the islands and hammocks surrounding Savannah, including Wilmington, Beaulieu, and Skidaway Island and Long Point Hammock. Whether the holiday decor is palms, shells, or feathers—or elegant collectible ornaments—there is a true seasonal flair. The homes' natural surroundings always play a part in the role of the Christmas decor.

This elegant home on Long Point Hammock overlooks the Wilmington River.

Twilight on the Hammock

At night this home takes on a special glow. Twenty-foot tall arbor vitae wrapped in twinkling lights flank the grand entrance in December. Gas lanterns cast a warm welcome for party guests.

Entertaining friends with warmth and grace is the spirit of hospitality at Christmas—definitely a true Savannah tradition.

The table is set with Spode china and paired with olive green and grapevine mossed trees, and hand-painted wine glasses.

Eggnog Pound Cake

1 cup butter
1 cup shortening
3 cups sugar
6 eggs
3 cups all-purpose flour
1 cup eggnog
1 cup flaked coconut
1 teaspoon lemon extract
1 teaspoon vanilla extract
1 teaspoon coconut extract
Whipped cream, for garnish
Nutmeg, for garnish

Preheat the oven to 325 degrees F. Cream together the butter and short-ening. Gradually add the sugar, beating well. Add the eggs one at a time, beating well after each addition. Using a spoon, add the flour to creamed mixture alternating with the eggnog. Stir in the coconut and flavorings and blend well.

Pour the batter into a well-greased and floured 10-inch pan. Bake at 325 degrees F for 1½ hours. Remove from the oven and allow to cool for 10 minutes before removing the cake from the pan. Top with whipped cream and sprinkle with grated nutmeg.

Skidaway Island Elegance

Skidaway Island is one of the most beautiful islands along the Georgia coastline, and is home to many who enjoy Low Country living at its best.

From the moment you enter this home, the warmth of the decor exudes both the elegance and beauty of the season.

The owners of this home decorate their tree with ornaments that have been lovingly collected over many years. A fuschia flowering Christmas cactus is cradled in a mid-century English tureen. The owner's grandmother always kept this plant in her home during the holidays The grouping of figurines on the chest are mid-19th century decorative pieces from England.

The formal monogrammed dinner service of American silver (above) dates from the 1920s. The individual covered bouillon cups were made by Well and Tree.

At right, the mid-19th century old English ironstone footbath is planed with pale yellow poinsettias. Ironstone plates and a pair of cut glass clarets flank a silver vase, and the mirror reflects the blue and white transferware opposite the dining table.

On the formal dining table, the antique goblets (that once belonged to Mary Byrd Mc-Carthy) and the American silver candlesticks by Shreve & Company are part of the sophisticated setting. The silver Christoffe French candelabras complete this traditional holiday table setting.

The centerpiece is made up of Christmas tree greenery and chartreuse roses woven together the length of the table.

C. H. Brown's Silver Shop

A favorite local antique silver collector Charles Brown decorates many trees around his shop during the holidays; one uses only rare coin silver as ornaments, and another is hung with antique baby cups. The one shown here features silver cups as ornaments.

Hosting an annual open house during the holidays, he serves his signature eggnog and his mother's decadent coconut cake. It is a much anticipated holiday party by the neighbors in the historic district, many of whom are avid silver collectors, too. With an exquisite table dressed with the finest antique silver, china, and linens, teamed with the Brown's infectious personality, this is a cherished party invitation.

Antique silver trophies line the mantel and are filled with masses of hypericum berries.

Beaulieu ⤳

Located on the Vernon River, the stately residences look as though they have been on this land for centuries, and many are historic; however, this grand home was built in 2005. The property was originally a part of the Beaulieu Plantation, which was a King's land grant dating from 1739.

This circa 1860 home was moved by barge to its current site on the Vernon River. These sparkly icicle ornaments in the window are about as close as the residents will get to snow in the South, but one can always dream.

The children's collection of nutcrackers (opposite page) are displayed on the kitchen mantel. Olive green felt Christmas trees, sewn by a folk artist, are strung along the fireplace. The buttons and thread add homespun details to the trees. Shiny acorn ornaments are hung along the yarn garland that drapes the mantel.

Strawberry Strata

This is a delightful dish to serve for a Christmas brunch. It is easy to fix and looks beautiful on your holiday table.

1 large loaf French bread, sliced
2 (8-ounce) packages cream cheese, cubed
12 eggs
2 cups half & half
6 tablespoons (¾ stick) butter, melted
½ cup maple syrup
Cinnamon
1 jar strawberry preserves
1 (16-ounce) container frozen sliced strawberries, thawed

The night before, place half the bread in a greased 9 x 13-inch dish. Place the cream cheese cubes on top of the bread and top with the remaining slices of bread. In a blender, mix the eggs, half & half, butter, and maple syrup. Pour the mixture over the bread slices and sprinkle generously with cinnamon. Refrigerate overnight. The next morning, remove from the refrigerator one hour before baking. Bake at 350 degrees F for 50 minutes. Before serving, heat the preserves and add the strawberry slices. Allow guests to pour the strawberry mixture over their portion. Serves 8.

Wilmington Island Simplicity

This lovely white room overlooking the Wilmington River is always decorated for the holidays with white hydrangea, Star of Bethlehem, and ferns.

A Christmas tree towers over the dining table, its branches draped with twig garland and tiny white lights. Enormous natural pinecones with silver deer moss tucked between the tips, and a natural centerpiece flanked with candles keep the look simple and calm.

Creating Holiday Magic

What began as a mother-and-daughter event twelve years ago is now a tradition that all three daughters and their friends look forward to annually. Gingerbread-themed invitations are sent out and the girls look forward to their Gingerbread House Party. Pretzel windows (below) are added to an artistic edible cottage.

The Magic Season is here - it's true,
for the gingerbread houses
are waiting for you!

We have lots of icing -
colorful candy, too.

Be ready to go -
you have lots to do!

Hope you can join us
in all the fun.

You'll have
quite a treasure
when all's
said and done!

Sunday
December 14th
2:00 - 4:30 p.m.
12 Tidewater Way

Pounds of candy (below) serve as sidewalks, doors, windows, and flower boxes. Everyone at this party will have sweet dreams tonight!

At the annual Savannah Harbor Gingerbread Village party at the Westin Hotel, a local chef, along with many other artisans, create the city of Savannah out of gingerbread and eighty pounds of royal icing. Historic downtown homes are recreated with black licorice ironwork; the Talmadge bridge is adorned with peppermint wreaths; and the dome of City Hall, both real and imagined, is covered with thin sheets of gold.

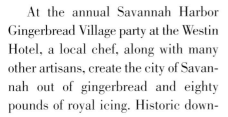

chapter eight

The Ford Plantation & the Low Country

In the 1930s, Henry Ford, the world's first billionaire, purchased a 1,800-acre estate just eighteen miles from Savannah and turned it into his part-time residence. The estate now showcases grand homes, horse stables, and exquisite nature sites, as well as a marina for boating and fishing, and biking and hiking trails. What a beautiful backdrop for the Christmas season!

December at the Ford Plantation offers oyster roasts along the banks of the Ogeechee River and wine tastings in the main plantation house, while a pianist plays holiday tunes.

Cisco (left) finds a special treat in his Christmas stocking at the stable!

In the 18th century much of the land along the Ogeechee River just south of Savannah was a rice plantation. In the 1930s Henry Ford turned these acres into a Southern winter retreat. The Ford House, now the main house in the plantation, has a gracious lawn and grand oak alleys.

The pool offered recreation for the Ford family, and remains a lovely feature on the grounds today. The grand lawn is perfect for afternoon oyster roasts during the month of December.

A handsome library (below) sets the stage for a cozy afternoon of reading beside a warm fire.

This stunning dining room features a flower composition of citrus, fatsia berries, eucalyptus seeds, hypericum berries, lilies, and Cherokee roses (the Georgia state flower). The elegance and natural beauty of the arrangement beautifully complements the room.

As one walks through this grand fairytale-like setting, it is easy to imagine the fabulous holiday parties which must have taken place at the Ford's retreat.

Just past the private entry gates of the Ford Plantation a welcome committee of beautiful horses stand tall in the grassy paddocks surrounded by white fencing. The Ford Plantation Equestrian Center offers a full-service boarding facility including a 22 stall barn. The grounds provide ten miles of forest riding trails, open meadows, and waterfront trails.

This local homeowner proudly displays his game from hunting trips all over the world in his trophy room (opposite). There are some big surprises for those who enter through this door; nevertheless, the tall Christmas tree and bright red poinsettias mark the holiday season.

Beaufort Ambience

Beaufort, founded in 1711, is a favorite small town in the South and a getaway destination for Savannahians. The town, nestled between Charleston, South Carolina, and Savannah is full of charm and historical holiday richness during the month of December. With typical small town hospitality of the local shops and gallery owners, quaint inns, and cozy cafes, the Christmas season is a joyous time in Beaufort.

The atmosphere of a Southern porch in Beaufort (opposite page) portrays contentment, a place to linger for a spell and enjoy the official "cocktail" of the South— iced sweet tea. Iced tea in the winter, you ask? Of course!

The tree (right) flourishes with ornaments made throughout the years by children, as well as a collection of nutcracker-themed ornaments.

Southerners have always loved having a music room in their house (above). It's a perfect area of the home to entertain while enjoying familiar holiday tunes.

Beaufort's Rhett House

The Rhett House Inn is located in the heart of Beaufort's historic district. The 9,000 square foot, 1820 antebellum plantation home welcomes guests from near and far during the holiday season.

Afternoon tea and wine in the evenings, is served on the verandah. And, upon request, gourmet picnics are prepared for guests—what a treat !

Baked Pimiento Cheese

This makes a wonderful party appetizer, or is great served with soup on a cold winter's night. For bacon lovers, you can also add crumbled, crispy-fried bacon before it goes in the oven.

1 (4-ounce) jar diced pimientos, drained
1½ cups mayonnaise
1 teaspoon Worcestershire sauce
1½ teaspoon finely grated onion
¼ teaspoon ground red pepper
1 (16-ounce) block sharp cheddar cheese, shredded

Stir together the first five ingredients in a large mixing bowl; stir in the shredded cheese. Spoon the mixture into a lightly greased two-quart baking dish. Bake at 350 degrees F for 20 minutes, or until bubbly. Serve with wheat crackers or a loaf of homemade bread.

Index

Index

Acknowledgments

We wish to thank the following people for help with this book: Phyllis Craft, Brooke Odom, Bethesda Academy for Boys, Wormsloe Plantation, Cindy and Joe Edwards, Adrian and John Robinson, Christine Hall, Meb and Hurley Ryan, Jane Coslick, Lee Ann and James Holcomb, Rhonda and Dow Hoffman, LeaAnne and Jeff Wallace, Donna and Tony Eichholz, Back in the Day Bakery, the Westin hotel, Theresa and Duncan Pindar, Erica and Tad Wilson, Susan and Steve Roberts, Leanne and Richard Dodd, Amy and Ashley Pinkney, Boo and John Kennedy, Charles H. Brown, Angela and Bill Coonce, Susan and Bill Lovett, McBrier and Michael Maloney, Carol and Ralph Moore, Elizabeth and Nicholas Dardes, Bari and Jacob Nunamaker, Ella's, Peggy and Skip Gillenwater, The Ford Plantation, The Rhett House Inn, Marc Jacobs, Hamilton Turner Inn, Diana and Craig Barrow, The Paris Market & Brocante, No. Four Eleven, Cathedral of St. John the Baptist, Wesley Monumental United Methodist Church, First Unitarian Church, St. John's Episcopal Church, Judy and Dan Bradley, Jane Johnson, the Lancaster Tree Farm, Kurt Oelschig, Oelschig Nursery, Julie Rubin, Gail and David Knopf, Diane Kaufman, Ryan and Kirsten Schiff, and the law firm of Inglesby, Falligant, Horne, Courington, & Chisholm.